D1320578

MIKE TROUT

BY PAUL HOBLIN

SportsZone

An Imprint of Abdo Publishing
abdopublishing.com

abdopublishing.com

Published by Abdo Publishing, a division of ABDO, PO Box 398166, Minneapolis, Minnesota 55439. Copyright © 2016 by Abdo Consulting Group, Inc. International copyrights reserved in all countries. No part of this book may be reproduced in any form without written permission from the publisher. SportsZone™ is a trademark and logo of Abdo Publishing.

Printed in the United States of America, North Mankato, Minnesota
042015
092015

THIS BOOK CONTAINS
RECYCLED MATERIALS

Cover Photo: G. Newman Lowrance/AP Images
Interior Images: G. Newman Lowrance/AP Images, 1; Peter Joneleit/Cal Sport Media/AP Images, 4; Paul Sancya/AP Images, 7; Rich Schultz/AP Images, 9; Steve Moore/AP Images, 10; Mike Janes/Four Seam Images/AP Images, 13; Larry Goren/Four Seam Images/AP Images, 15; Chris Carlson/AP Images, 16; Chris O'Meara/AP Images, 19; Nick Wass/AP Images, 21; Alex Gallardo/AP Images, 22, 27; Jeff Roberson/AP Images, 25; Bill Nichols/AP Images, 29

Editor: Nick Rebman.
Series Designer: Craig Hinton

Library of Congress Control Number: 2015931749

Cataloging-in-Publication Data
Hoblin, Paul.
 Mike Trout: MLB superstar / Paul Hoblin.
  p. cm. -- (Playmakers)
Includes bibliographical references and index.
ISBN 978-1-62403-842-6
1. Trout, Mike, 1991- --Juvenile literature. 2. Baseball players--United States--Biography--Juvenile literature. 3. Major League Baseball (Organization)--Juvenile literature.   I. Title.
796.357092--dc23
[B]   2015931749

TABLE OF CONTENTS

Mike Trout

CHAPTER 1

THE YOUNGEST AND THE BEST

Mike Trout stood at home plate. He lifted the bat over his shoulder. Derek Jeter was on second base. Jeter had always been Trout's favorite player. And now they were teammates in the 2014 All-Star Game.

When the pitch came, Trout hit the ball hard. It crashed into the fence in right field. Trout sprinted around the bases. He slid safely into third. And Jeter scored a run on Trout's hit.

Mike Trout launches a ball during the 2014 season.

Jeter was 40 years old. He was one of the best players of his time. But he was playing his last season. Trout was only 22 years old. People said he was the future of baseball.

Mike played four seasons at Millville High School. In that time, he struck out only 17 times.

Mike had always been good for his age. When he was eight years old, he played against 10-year-olds. When he was 10, he played against 12-year-olds. By the time he was a freshman at Millville High School in New Jersey, he was playing on the varsity team.

Mike was good at every game he tried. On the basketball court, he grabbed lots of rebounds. And that was when he was not dunking. During his freshman year he also played football. He was so good that his coaches begged him to keep playing. They wanted him to be their quarterback. Mike had other plans, though. He wanted to focus on his favorite sport.

Trout, *left*, talks to Derek Jeter before the 2014 All-Star Game.

Since he was little, baseball had been the game he liked best. Back then, he hit Wiffle balls in his backyard. Sometimes he could not find any Wiffle balls. So he hit rocks instead.

Mike's dad, Jeff, had been a minor league player. So no one was shocked that Mike was good at baseball. But they were amazed at how good he was. During his senior year of high school, his batting average was .531. He broke the New Jersey single-season record with 18 home runs. He did it in only 81 at-bats.

In the majors, Mike plays center field. But back in high school he did some pitching, too. During his junior year, he struck out 124 batters in only 70 innings. He can throw a fastball more than 90 miles per hour.

Mike was clearly a great player. But not many people knew about him. He grew up in the northeastern United States. Baseball scouts do not usually spend much time there. After all, kids in the Northeast have to deal with cold winters. That means they have shorter playing seasons. So they do not get to practice as much as kids from the South. Many scouts figured that players from New Jersey were not worth watching.

Luckily, one scout did believe in Mike. His name was Greg Morhardt. He worked for the Los Angeles Angels. He convinced the Angels that Mike could be a major league superstar.

Mike smiles for the cameras after being chosen by the
Los Angeles Angels in 2009.

But the Angels had a problem. They could not pick a player
until late in the first round of the 2009 Major League Baseball
(MLB) draft. So they waited. And Mike waited. Other teams kept
drafting other players. Finally, with the twenty-fifth pick, the
Angels chose Mike.

Most teams in the league had a chance to take Mike. But
they chose other players instead. These teams soon realized
they had made a big mistake.

Mike Trout

CHAPTER 2

MINOR LEAGUE MARVEL

Mike Trout was now a professional baseball player. But he was not yet a major leaguer. First he had to play well in the minor leagues. That is exactly what he did.

Trout's first stop was the Arizona Rookie League. In his first game as a pro, he made it safely to first base six times. In 39 games, Trout had a .360 batting average.

Trout got his first major league experience during the 2011 season.

Clearly, Trout was ready for a new challenge. He was sent to a higher league. He played for the Cedar Rapids Kernels. Trout quickly became one of the best players in the Midwest League. In fact, he became the best player. After hitting .362, he was named the Most Valuable Player (MVP). He was also named the Prospect of the Year.

The minor leagues can be tough. Players often have to get up early in the morning. They spend a lot of time on the road. Trout's parents wanted to make life easier for their son. They brought him laundry detergent, toilet paper, and bed sheets. They even brought him food.

Trout was more than a great hitter. He was a great all-around player. As a former star pitcher, he had a strong arm. As a center fielder, he was fast. He ran down fly balls and line drives that most players could not reach. When he hit a ground ball, he could run to first base in under four seconds.

Trout was not perfect, of course. But he learned from his mistakes. One time, his coach yelled at him for not hustling. Later in the game, his teammate got a base hit. Trout was

Trout played for the Scottsdale Scorpions, a team in the Arizona Fall League, in 2011.

on first base, but not for long. He hustled around second base. Then he ran around third. Then he ran all the way to home plate!

Trout's teammates might have been jealous of his success if he had just been talented. But he was humble. And he was fun to hang out with. Instead of being jealous, they rooted for Trout. They cheered as loudly as he cheered for them.

In 2011 Trout played for the Arkansas Travelers. He won the minor league Player of the Year award. By now, no one was surprised.

Trout and his minor league teammates often ate dinner together. One of Trout's favorite foods was Dominican rice. He could eat 2 pounds (0.91 kilograms) of rice during a single meal.

The Los Angeles Angels were ready to see what Trout could do. He finally got to play in the major leagues. But he did not stay there long. For the first time in his career, Trout struggled. In 2011 he played 40 games for the Angels. He hit just .220.

The Angels sent him back to the minor leagues at the start of the 2012 season. It was disappointing for Trout. He told the team he would work as hard as he could in the minors. He

Trout runs the bases during his rookie season.

hoped to earn another chance at playing for the Angels later in the year.

He did exactly that. Trout played only 20 games for the Salt Lake Bees. In that time, he hit .403. The Angels decided they wanted Trout back in their lineup.

This time, Trout was prepared. But the other major league teams were not prepared for him.

16   Mike Trout

CHAPTER 3

ROOKIE OF THE CENTURY

By the end of June 2012, Mike Trout had made a name for himself. He led the league in batting average. He led the league in stolen bases. And he was selected to play in the All-Star Game.

As usual, Trout did more than hit. He also played amazing defense.

On June 27, the Angels played the Baltimore Orioles. The Orioles' batter stepped up to the plate.

Trout blasts a home run during his rookie season.

He crushed a ball to deep center field. Trout raced after it. The ball started to zoom over the fence. But Trout jumped high into the air. He twisted his body. He reached over the fence. Somehow he snagged the ball in his glove.

It was an incredible catch. When Trout landed, he saw that the ball was in his glove. He could hardly believe it. Neither could anyone else. Trout let out an excited whoop. Then he did the same thing as everyone else in the stadium. He turned to the giant scoreboard. He wanted to watch the replay.

Trout stole 49 bases in 2012. He was caught stealing just five times.

This was his first home run–robbing catch of the season. But it was not his last. On August 5, the Angels played the Seattle Mariners. Once again a batter hit a towering fly ball. And once again Trout timed his jump perfectly. He snatched the baseball out of the air. The Angels' pitcher yelled, "Wow!"

Trout steals second base in a 2013 game against the Tampa Bay Rays.

Trout had perhaps his best game on September 8. He started the game by belting a home run. He finished it by leaping over the fence. This time he took a home run away from slugger Prince Fielder.

Miguel Cabrera won the MVP in both 2012 and 2013. Trout took second place both years.

It did not matter whether Trout was using his bat or his glove. He spent the 2012 season helping his team win. The Angels had not been doing well before Trout joined them. They had won six games and lost 14. Once Trout joined the team, the Angels won 83 games. They lost only 59.

Trout was more than good. He was better than just about any 20-year-old in history. Trout was the youngest ever to join the 30–30 club. That happens when a player hits 30 home runs and steals 30 bases in a season.

At the end of the season, Trout was named Rookie of the Year. He also took second place in MVP voting. Many people believed he was the best all-around player in the world.

Trout reaches over the wall to rob a Baltimore Orioles batter of a home run.

Mike Trout

CHAPTER 4

FUTURE LEGEND

After his historic rookie season, Mike Trout went home. He was now a millionaire. He could have bought a huge house. Instead, he wanted to live in his parents' basement.

After all, the basement had everything he needed. It had a Ping-Pong table. It had a dartboard. And there were tons of video games. Trout spent his off-season the same way he had spent his childhood. He competed against his friends and family.

Trout makes a leaping catch in a 2014 game at Angel Stadium.

When the next season began, Trout picked up right where he left off. He kept hitting for both average and power. He kept stealing bases. And he kept making spectacular plays in the field.

Trout has been timed as he runs the bases. He moves at more than 20 miles per hour. That means he could almost keep up with a car as it moves through a city.

For the second year in a row, he was named to the All-Star team. His success on the field was even more impressive than the year before. Opposing teams had all winter to find holes in Trout's game. But they could not come up with many. They knew that he was a lowball hitter. So they tried throwing higher pitches. The problem was, Trout had a good eye at the plate. He did not swing at the high pitches.

Trout finished the year with a .323 average. He also took more walks than he had in his rookie season. He batted in more runs, too. It was another great year.

Trout holds up his MVP trophy after the 2014 All-Star Game.

Still, he was not satisfied. He had won individual awards and honors. But his team had not won enough games. To him, the most important goal was not personal success. He wanted his team to reach the playoffs.

It would not be easy. Trout had put together two of the finest seasons in baseball history. Even so, the Angels had not made the playoffs.

On June 27, 2014, the Angels played the Kansas City Royals. In the first inning, Trout hit a 489-foot home run. It was the longest home run ever hit by an Angels player. The previous Angels record was held by Vladimir Guerrero. He hit a 484-foot home run in 2006.

At the beginning of 2014, Trout was in a major slump. From April 29 to May 19, he hit only .164. He struck out 24 times. Some people thought pitchers had finally discovered how to get him out.

Then he snapped out of his slump. It happened just as suddenly as it began. During the next month and a half, a red-hot Trout hit .387.

Even better, the Angels were winning. There was just one problem. The Angels were stuck in second place. At the All-Star break, the Angels had the second-best record in baseball. Unfortunately, they played in the same division as the Oakland A's. And the A's had the best record in baseball.

Finally in late August, the Angels moved past the A's. Once they did, they did not look back. The Angels finished the regular

On June 7, 2014, Trout hit a grand slam to help the Angels win.
Jered Weaver, *right*, dumps water on Trout after the game.

season with the best record in baseball. They had 98 wins and

only 64 losses. Finally, Trout was going to the playoffs.

Unfortunately, the Angels were not in the playoffs for long.

They may have been the best team in the regular season. But

Trout agreed to let his high school sell T-shirts with his name on them. All the money made from these shirts goes to the school and its students.

the Kansas City Royals were the better team in the playoffs. The Royals swept the Angels, three games to zero. Trout hit a home run in the last game. But by then it was too late.

The Angels' season had ended. Still, there were reasons to feel optimistic. For one thing, the Angels had won a lot of games. More important, they still had Trout on their team. In 2014, he hit the most home runs of his young career. He also took home his first MVP award.

By now, everyone in the baseball world knows there is nothing Mike Trout cannot do.

Trout hits the ball during his MVP season of 2014.

FUN FACTS AND QUOTES

- As a kid, Mike Trout was a batboy for the high school team.

- Greg Morhardt, the scout who discovered Trout, played in the minor leagues. Trout's father was one of Morhardt's teammates.

- Trout hit well at every minor league level. His overall minor league batting average was .342.

- Trout's favorite restaurant is back home in Millville. It is called Jim's Lunch. Trout can eat six mini hamburgers in one sitting.

- Trout says hello to the home plate umpire at the beginning of each game. He also taps the catcher with his bat. He wishes both of them a good game.

- Trout's nickname is the Millville Meteor. The name started as a joke on Wikipedia. Soon fans and writers were using it, too.

WEBSITES

To learn more about Playmakers, visit **booklinks.abdopublishing.com**. These links are routinely monitored and updated to provide the most current information available.

GLOSSARY

all-around player
A player who is good at hitting, running, throwing, and catching.

batting average
A player's number of hits divided by the number of at-bats.

draft
The time when each team gets to select new players.

hustling
Moving quickly.

minor leagues
A lower level of baseball where players work on improving their skills before they reach the major leagues.

MVP
An award given to the best player in each league.

off-season
The time of year when there are no games.

playoffs
A set of games after the regular season that decides which team will be the champion.

scout
A person who travels around looking for good young players.

slump
A period of time when a player is not doing well.

stolen base
The act of running from one base to another during a pitch, not during a hit.

varsity
The top level of high school sports.

INDEX

FURTHER RESOURCES

Editors of Sports Illustrated Kids Magazine. *Sports Illustrated Kids Full Count: Top 10 Lists of Everything in Baseball.* New York: Time Home Entertainment Inc., 2012.

Jacobs, Greg. *The Everything Kids' Baseball Book: From Baseball History to Player Stats—With Lots of Home Run Fun in Between!* Avon, MA: Adams Media, 2010.

Kelley, James. *Baseball.* New York: DK Pub., 2005.